I FEEL YOUR DOUGHNUT PAIN

over-the-counter poems
to inspire the next counter-culture revolution

STEPHEN ROXBOROUGH

OPTIMYSTIC PRESS

Copyright © 2020 by Stephen Roxborough

All rights reserved. No part of this book may be used or reproduced in any manner whatsoever without express written permission from the publisher except in the case of brief quotations embodied in critical articles and reviews.

Stephen Roxborough – I Feel Your Doughnut Pain
ISBN 978-0-578-66339-5 (paperback: alk. paper)

1. Poetry. I. Roxborough, Stephen. II. I Feel Your Doughnut Pain.
2. American history

Library of Congress Control Number: 2020906259

Design, art direction & typography: Milo Duffin and Stephen Roxborough

Printed in La Vergne, USA

to those who don't approve the status quo
who see every power grab
who oppose twisted logic to suppress & control
who ask hard questions & seek fair answers
& who refuse to be silenced
or surrender
to the forces of dark hearts

TABLE OF CONTENTS

MISSIVES & MISSLES — 1-38
we must first acknowledge the problem

CHANTS & RANTS — 41-73
pendulum swings between outrage & calm

EXHALES & DOVETAILS — 77-108
pain is a reflection of our disconnect

USA: PSA — 111-131
education: learning to ask better questions

PRAYERS & FLARES — 135-162
illumination & manifestation for the nation

when he wrote *the fall of america*

poems from 1965 to 1971
allen ginsberg said he was too late
amerika had already fallen

this book arrives 50 years later & amerika
is still falling
    so accustomed to descent
  we now fall fearlessly as if immune
to the consequences
    perhaps we've become
more callous to the costs
or we don't believe rock bottom
is ever really coming

as experts in the department of decline
amerikans have raised the genre
to a fine art
    how to plummet with grace
  not brace yourself for impact
ignore all warnings
blissfully bounce without resistance
deftly slide by obstacles & roll
with unholy momentum

then how to slyly spin the misstep
the trip the stumble the slip
the collapse cover-up stagger blame
salute with a hollywood smile
& try to find a way
to bounce back
better

MISSIVES & MISSILES

dear amerika you've lost

your focus your mojo your edge your drive
but most of all you've lost your zen
your finger pointing
at the moon

you've become perfectly lazy & complacent
you're totally disinterested & easily distracted
you don't believe in practice or excellence
or the answerless question

walk the path
observe your breath

you keep looking for the easy way out
a few magic beans or cheap fairytale ending
you don't believe in ritual or repetition
you dream the lottery will save you
from self-improvement & hard work ha!

walk the path
observe your breath

ice cream hot dogs football
& the 18th century internal combustion engine
have failed you
              the perfect irony of inventing
perma-press & instant mashed potatoes!

walk the path
observe your breath

dear amerika you lost your humility
trying to avoid self-discipline
the world is not your oyster anymore
amerika you are not who

you think you are
or were
but that's okay
sometimes it's helpful to get lost
to find yourself

walk the path
observe your breath

sport art service music cooking
healing designing listening washing
teaching negotiation
advertising leadership
the potential for zen
in everything
                      even amerika

walk the path
observe your breath

toast

here's to the beautiful perpetual
national stupor of lost & founding fathers
here's to their patri-idiotic bluster

how we brainwash ourselves
in collective ignorance
riding on the coattails of rewritten history
& the lies we tell ourselves to sustain
our self-esteem
& maintain
        the great experiment
        of the greatest show on earth

we're doomed to repeat the worst parts of ourselves
we're doomed to repeat the worst parts of ourselves
because we all feel the need to believe
what we force-feed us
& ratings depend on creating
a bigger better drama

so here's to our brains pickled battered & deep fried
under the cover-up of this toxic
nationalistic stupor

here's to the beautiful perpetual
national stupor of lost & founding fathers
a haze so thick
you can't cut it with a sharp wit

the united states of obliviousness

the united states of amnesia
it was something we forgot
to begin to remember

the united states of anesthesia
with ism after ism
we put ourselves to sleep

the united mistakes of amerika
foolish war is the new occupation
let's build a tar-baby plantation

the divided hates of amerika
we can't even agree to disagree
who we should abhor more

the united states of mediocrity
with a monopoly on baloney
we can't wait to lower the bar

the united states of capitalism
the modern mode of feudalism
& the home of disposable shopping

the united states of lost in space
a crazy race away from home
maybe someplace we'll save face

the united states of WTF
dumbing down is numbing down
bubble-gumming us alt-round

the indicted states of amerika
you're busted! to feed the greed
of prison for profit

the united states of nostalgia
she ain't what she used to be
& maybe baby she never was

the united states of interest rates
a rollercoaster flood from chinatown
so far underwater we're upside down

the united states of fear & loathing
it's a love hate control-for-your-soul
heaven-can-wait kinda thing

the united states of dystopia
our solutions make bigger problems
& we're addicted to solutions

the united states of never enough
where the needy are greedy
& the greedy are the greediest of all

the shortsighted states of amerika
buildings crumbling bridges tumbling
the infrastructure of bumbling & bungling

the united states of miasma
a wretched net of haze weighs down
the brains & engines of ingenuity

the united states of no-fault hate
may all your transgressions be forgiven
& driven deep into the folds of history

the united states of amnesia
it was something we forgot
to begin to remember

bumper-sticker landscape

amerika: home of the atomic bomb since 1945
amerika: built to last on stolen land
amerika: a kinder gentler racism
amerika: we think we invented everything
amerika: hoodwinked by tobacco drugs & oil
amerika: only we're dumb enough
                        to drop the big one
amerika: where guns are job one
amerika: my button is bigger than your button
amerika: we starve artists & poor people
amerika: too expensive for average citizens
amerika: we used to make things here
amerika: drowning in first world problems
amerika: our founding fathers were slave owners
amerika: home of the incredible shrinking dollar
amerika: don't mess with texas
amerika: would you like some fries
                        with your genocide?
amerika: where middle class dreams go to die
amerika: we traded our souls for toys
amerika: every day a new normal
amerika: we're building more prisons!
amerika: nothing can stop us! unfortunately
amerika: we're dumber than we look
amerika: not as crowded as india or china
amerika: but our beer is getting better
amerika: it could always be worse

why amerika?

C is soft curvy accepting
feminine friendly 2 points linear latin
careful classic cautious civil circle
symbol for carbon copyright
celsius average
chippewa cherokee choctaw
crow cree cheyenne
cleveland chicago clarksdale
cagney carlin carson
crosby coco
cobain coppola cruise
cher cheese cake carrot corn
coca cola capital
& vitamin sunshine
                whereas
                      K has angles
              edge power convergence
   non-linear greek masculine kappa
                symbol for potassium
       kelvin king strikeout black ink
          kryptonite kilo thousand
            kesey kafka philip k dick
                 kellogg kardasian
             kevorkian koons kroc
  kill kiss knife ketchup karma kink
    kook kayo klutz key kickback
            kingpin kidnap kazoo
                  short for OK
                        KKK
                     & K street

dear amerika (once again)

i want my money back
those taxes i paid from all the years
i slaved

that moolah you squandered on war
& secret CIA adventures
all those dead presidents you burned through
building military toys & imaginary walls
to keep out the mongolian hoards

how you overfunded the police state
to beat up the poor & bail out
the rich

you built the bus that drove us
into the bankruptcy ditch
& now we're owned by the chinese
i paid through the nose to watch this movie
but i never expected a full house
of congressional clowns
could dismantle my bill of rights

roll up your sleeves & get to work
the party's over

time for a female bull-moose square deal
or do we simply buy finer pillows
& re-dream the amerikan nightmare

i'm torn between my ugly baby
& your dirty bathwater

they call him the dumpster

mister pee humpty trumpty agent orange
cry baby birther boy the donald
putin's puppet
man baby chubby nubby
mister comb-over the pussy grabber
the groper-in-chief
tangerine jesus
prima donald president perk
the tweeter-in-chief
mister locker room talk
old king coal
baby fingers darth trump
the banana republican
the bully pulpit bully
sexist fascist racist pig fake president
the you're fired dude
liar cheater pretender-in-chief
the last of the old white privilege guys
with short memory & long ties
putin's poodle
small hands donald dupe
captain chaos tweetledum
putin's bitch richie rich
the reverse robin hood
forest trump
donny moscow stuperman
the tweester the toxic avenger
the racist-in-chief
the fraud of fifth avenue
treasonous trump
don the con

some say it was the best of times

but the times says
it's the worst of times

some say it's a tale of two buildings
the tower in moscow that never got built
& a skyscraper in nyc named 666

we got secret meetings about private emails
& how to make an election go off the rails
we got a russian weightlifter & the president's daughter
we got over 3 million pieces of evidence
from the president's fixer
we got a porn star in the president's cookie jar
we got witnesses flipping like flapjacks
we got a witch-hunt that keeps catching witches
we got tax cuts for the rich to get richer
we got a senior who's a cheater & a junior who's a loser
we got spygate & lie-gate & rick gates
we got middle eastern billions
mixed up with the president's minions
we got innocent kids that can't see their mothers
we got a piggybank charity & a wealth
of immaturity
we got love-letter words for a killer
with a button & a bomb
his tweets alone enough to leave you breathless
cause we got no metrics for trumpian ethics

& yet still some say move along
there's nothing wrong

nothing really to see here

shhhhhhhhh...

i don't want him to think i would
ever want to think about him

i don't want him to think i'd ever
make a stink about him

he's a big wheel of a deal in his mind
thinks he's god's gift for all-time

he doesn't have the grace to save face
or to fall tastefully from grace

he'll probably just implode one day
hope he doesn't explode your way

when they catch him they'll cuff em
& rough em & make sure he goes away

because he adores only himself
he gets smaller every day

someone else might pardon him
but really there's no excuse for him

because he mostly only loves himself
we'll make sure he goes away

dear amerika the swamp is deep &

wide & you'll never cross without
wings & a guide

it's a global sewer of alligators
& dirty rats spreading the disease
of desire with bribes
& kickbacks to fat cats

the crocodiles are large & in charge
of the pyramid scheme
in god we trust plus allah & buddha
& oil & soybeans & the big wheels
of the war machine

the swamp's grown too big to control
or ignore
      you can tell by the slime
seeping under your door
& it's climbing the walls of your cages
leaking through the seams
of your rages

are you mad enough yet? or just
too numb to regret

there's a dark slick making us sick
on any ocean you're in
& right now i'm not in the mood
for a swim

they painted	**the white**	**house black**
embraced	the dark	side
anointed	themselves	with powers
regenerated	reptilian	brains
ravenous	for blood	and gore
cleansed	the world	with brainwashing
force fed	the masses	half truths
crucified	candor with	torture
transplanted	seeds of	terror
harvested	amber waves	of fear
recalibrated	the scales	of justice
made	a mockery of	democracy
rubbed	our noses	in their patriot act
lied & spied	on us	for freedom
liberated	innocents	with shock & awe
we are weak	and you	are strong
we are lost	and you	are found
we are children	and you	are president
	good lord	vader
	protect us	
	from ourselves	

adding up revised adages

socialism is the opiate of the masses
give me internet or give me death
speak softly but carry a big joy stick

& the robots shall inherit the earth

the road of mediocrity is paved
with the path of least resistance

give me convenience or give me death
a discount on entropy isn't all
it's cracked up to be

time to let go when the cure
is worse than the disease

eat like you've given up
relax like there's no tomorrow
dance like a blind pig
on a peg-legged date

time is the great equalizer
either time or ketchup

we have nothing to fear but
our ignorance
try not to choke on your own babble

give me entropy & give me death

somewhere in the middle

of the united states of mediocrity
smack dab in the kidney of the heartland
where the salt of the earth
depends on the sky
to scrape & root out a living

where pesticides wage genocide
& there's only one religion one sport
one political party one marriage
you can count on
   the almighty weather
& everything depends on barometric pressure
because they're not buying quantum entanglement
subatomic energy & the changing waves
of vibration
yet

unlike the first stewards of this land
who knew a great dance could make rain
a steady drumbeat could summon spirits
& a 10-day chant would change
the world
   these hard-boiled sun-grizzled
stiff rigid farmers still believe
the lives of the rich will create a better dream
& herd their camels through
the eye of the needle

unbeknownst to them a billion butterflies
have already fluttered their wings in brazil
as ice sheets the size of countries
break away
   & a hundred billion hearts are opening
as the land the sky & ocean are speaking

if only they'd turn off their machines
to hear it

if only they'd tune their internal channel
to receive it
if only they'd discover
the opening within is greater than
the universe without

we're puttin on the fear tonight

dressin up & gettin outta here
because no one is safe
the windows the doors
hell they might even come
through the floors

fear is the best of what we do
fear is our newest secret passion
what a captivating fashion
to keep that stranglehold on you

fear is the perfect tool
an instant transfusion of delusion
fear makes nothing right
fear makes everyone uptight
breeds chaos doubt & confusion

fear gets more twisted in your head
there's no end to its dark illusion
makes you beg for more control
makes you dream of a grassy knoll
makes you dubious of interpol
fear gives you a billion reasons
to commit treason in any season

so tonight we're puttin on the fear
dressin up & gettin outta here
buy you ten shots of whatever they got
toast you a dose of friendly paranoia

it's hip it's hot it's all the rage
we'll dance till we drop
then shift into another phase
don't go anywhere just stay right here
we got everything you want
we got everything you fear

amerika

named after an italian
put on the map by a german
colonized by the british
revolutionized by taxation
advertised by franklin
bought the river from napoleon
genocide by jackson
made ugly by slavery
emancipated by abraham
uncivilized by civil war
won the west with winchester
heard singing by whitman
made beautiful by a feminist
greeted masses by lazarus
improvised by jelly roll
given voice by guthrie
taught to swim by dylan
split atoms for annihilation
defiled by pollution
blinded by religion
made uglier by money
dumbed down by drugs
flooded with debt
set aflame by greed
monitored by screens
married to the mob
& blessed by god
through a russian jew
o amerika dear amerika
you've come a long way baby
from virgin forest to plastic sea
as if original turtle island
wasn't enough for
you & me

the new upgraded extended-play colossus

give me your wired & screen-addicted
your ice cream & meme afflicted
give me your lovelorn soft-porn blue pill
credit card bill run-of-the-mill lonely heart
outcast redneck weapons expert

give me your befuddled masses
from here to parnassus
give me your poor your raconteur
your amor with delusions of grandeur
give me your racist your homophobe
your feeble sheeple zombie
& your born-again ex-smoker
self-righteous cross-dressing nazi

give me your obese your obtuse your confused
your bipolar soldier your unholy roller
your abused & refused
& your dumbed-down small-town
renowned political clown

give me your old broken cowboys
& past their prime playboys
give me your teenage street corner medicine men
& your two-faced corporate ladder climbers
give me your washed-up athletes
& your brainwashed wall street elite

give me your heartless & your homeless
give me your helpless your idiots your savants
your servants & masters of unspeakable acts
give me your wannabes your rabies
your rabbis
your thalidomide babies
your molesters your protesters
your drunks & monks your seekers

your preachers your teachers & priests
give me your anorexics your dyslexics
your geeks & freaks
& your walking antiques

give me your bloated white privilege
& your ink jet black activist
give me your brown bag brownie
your yellow fever yellow & your refugee red

give me your screaming magenta
your hot pink & your half-dead
give me your blueblood & greenbacks
your bureaucrat gray & rita hayworth ginger
your glam & glitter your gold & silver
give me your sun-kissed orange
& your smoker's lung ochre
give me your imperfect purple
& your perfectly mediocre
give me your rainbow boho hobo
& give me everything to go

give me the world's biggest melting pot
give me all the colors in your crayon box
give me a taste of freedom
& a shot of liberty
give me a chaser of memory eraser
then deliver me with a strong punch
of real history
give me the whole fucking lot
forgive my temper tempest
you see i'm amerika
the greedy sot
so god bless you all
but goddamn gimme gimme gimme
give me everything you got

our lady of perpetual disappointment

the saint of all unfulfilled dreams & desires
patron to the lazy mediocre & easily confused
comfort to the directionally challenged
& habitual lottery losers

            salve for the forgotten
      the disenfranchised & the eternal burn
of unrequited love

benefactor for the ugly & overweight
the repeatedly dying & dieting
the failing & the afraid
the unwashed & uneducated
the slow thinkers & the fast foodies
the starving artists & the passed over
oboe players
        the greedy thief & the lifetime prisoner
the honest politician & the dishonest priest
the non-violent fighter & the warlord pacifist
the forgotten the tortured the bullied
the ostracized the outcast
the lost & the unlucky

our lady of perpetual disappointment
will hear your obstructions
listen to your problems
she lets you vent about your life
she absorbs these vibrations
& allows you to let them go
she agrees & consents
she authorizes you to make room
for something more positive in your life

always concurs you must find
your own way & grow
at your own pace

dear amerika have you tried

everything else yet
because we're long overdue
for doing the right thing
                       for putting education
over indoctrination & finally teaching the truth
about your history or is it our history
i'm not sure we have the stomach to own it
before we examine it

with genocide herbicide fratricide apartheid
& thalidomide it's not very pretty
did someone mention slavery?

we got wars we can't pay for
we got storms we can't afford
we got astronomical medical bills
& pills that never cure our ills
& everyone's waiting for
the big one to drop

we got big business big pharma big karma
big tobacco big oil big banks big wigs big hats
big earthquakes big storms big sugar big balls
big data big deals big meal deals
big ego big bird big show big fish big gun big fun
big prisons big brother big dicks big ships
big religion & big apocalypse
how come you never hear about big poetry?

dear amerika you can't drain the swamp
because it's a part of human nature
but we can expose it & own it
& not let it take over
         teach your children well amerika
how to choose education over indoctrination

the days of cookie-cutter factory schools
making human robots are terminated

dear amerika elevate our thoughts
& heal our liberal arts
teach our children to quiet their minds
& expand their hearts
before the fated complicated days
of artificial intelligence take over

i do not pledge allegiance

to any flag for which it stands
because to grant a symbol too much power
makes me feel uncomfortable & stupid

as if regurgitating a few grandiose words
gives them my permission to wage
war on people & planet
because i will not stand for that
or the national anthem
another glorification of weapons & war
amerika's most lucrative export

i will also not give this government
blind faith for all their anti-constitutional
human rights reducing acts & policies

their obvious racial & corporate bias
their endless gravy train for gluttonous banks
their apathy toward the poor & homeless
their lack of alarm for universal
healthcare & higher education
their denial & disinterest in ecology
& their unflagging support
of the uberwealthy

& i outright refuse to swallow
anymore of their mindless repetitious
brainwashing twisted hero distortion
for liberty & justice for all
rah rah blah blah
amen

given enough time she said

you could get used to anything
you mean he said like the classic frog
in the ever-increasing
heating pot

like prison or clutter or homelessness
or bad government she said
like the patriot act or NSA spying
or cameras
in refrigerators he said

like cameras in the street
& bugs in your computers she said
like bad air & bad water &
no universal healthcare he said

like climate change & polluted food
& mediocre music she said
like traffic jams & inflated prices
& daylight savings &
unaffordable housing he said

like failing education & endless war
lead in your drinking water
& a government that doesn't care
she said

& a government that
doesn't care

amerika doesn't care about health care

she's fat & bloated
she's diabetic arthritic unathletic
& heart disease is on its way
she could use a bi-pass or two
maybe three or four
but who's counting? because

amerika doesn't care about health care

her yo-yo diet of dead animals
& refined sugar
has attacked her liver
given her cancer
& they say if only we could throw
more money at it
we could kill that serial killer
but money builds a labyrinth bureaucracy
of paper pushers & fund raisers
while prevention is never
mentioned

amerika doesn't care about health care

she only wants more money
her system fueled by capitalism
& choking on itself
because you can't eat money
but a love for money
will eat you alive

dear amerika you were recently

downgraded from a full
to a flawed democracy

& i can't say that surprises me
because it's been a long time
since we were full of democracy

government of the people
by the people & for the people
seems a distant dream
                         hard to believe
a republican wrote & spoke those words
but now amerika we're floating
in the same shaky boat
as poland
mongolia & italy

you've lost trust & participation
& your flaws outnumber
your assets

we're all falling on a banana peel
called greed
                 while the future
       keeps slipping
further away

don't trust anything instant

dear amerika you've gone soft & lazy
& lost in a vortex of disinterest
your lack of compassion & culture
is killing you
one bad direction at a time

your deep-fried doughboy double patty
triple scoop secret sauce
butterscotch midnight snack
supersize heart-attack
unlimited buffet of instant gratification
& perpetual disappointment
isn't enough anymore

you wanna become millionaires
before you know the value of a trillion

damn amerika we have no business
counting that high or expecting instant wisdom
instant weight-loss instant oatmeal
or instant karma
                    we've even lost the line
that tells us when we've crossed the line

                don't trust anything instant
          because nothing's constant
you get no shortcuts
to lasting convenience
or comfortable conscience
it's a matter of do-the-work-first amerika

but you wanna become billionaires
before you become millionaires
& you wanna spend like a government
with an endless line of credit

but it's too late to pretend
you got nothing to defend except

you might be too lazy & soft & lost
to comprehend how to transcend
the structure of the culture embedded
with thirst & lust & the easy greed
of drive-thru ambition

damn amerika you can't microwave
or enslave or pave the road
to success
                    no don't trust anything instant
        because nothing is constant
& good things take time
most good things take time

dear amerika your slip

is showing & you fell from grace
a long time ago

your immune system compromised
your constitution weakened
& your tooth missing for decades

your eye-shadow running your bags sagging
your energy half-mast flagging

your stockings ripped your shoes don't fit
& your enlarged irregular heart
just doesn't seem to be in it

you're on anti-depressants & painkillers
with violent or catatonic side-effects

your coat of many colors has split
slashes & gashes & gaping despairs
the edges of your immaculate material frayed
& all your states of mind
coming further apart at the seams

you've been battered & bruised
neglected rejected & abused by many
for the few & still you look
like a dream to much of the world

yes even still millions & millions
line up for the remote lottery chance
just to dance with you

& maybe find a better home
in your tired occupied arms

word salad war

this war of words we wage
against coherence & reason & resolve we rage
                    world war 4
            has already begun
        already inside your door
without bombs or guns
on all your screens
with cutting
tongues
an asymmetrical assault
on common sense & truth

we chop   chop   the things we love
into smaller   & smaller   bits
then trade them   for a   fraction
the key to dissatisfaction
we slice & dice the absurd
    mix in the whole dictionary
of contradictory words
stir in the hatred & unrelated
& pour on the frustrated
                then we toss it into the air
            before we throw it at each other
we don't care where it sticks
                we're always onto
        the next battle
structure & grammar be damned
            we just need another sound-byte
                    to dominate the fight

something irreverent & hard hitting
something cool yet never satisfies
something that always leaves us
wanting more

dear amerika your guns

are killing you
day after day slowly but surely
tearing apart the fabric of your families
& freedoms
                    stitch by stitch
          tugging at your sacred
second amendment
thread
& leaving you
with holes in your hearts

in schools concerts churches hospitals
offices cinemas shopping malls
gas stations synagogues
grocery stores &
sidewalks in neighborhoods
& towns where you live & play

as if this the new norm
to shield a bulletproof constitution
business as usual for the flag-waving
weapons trade & militarized
society
                that bribes lawmakers
        to uphold a tattered constitution
to protect ourselves
from ourselves

wound up in a death spiral

wounded bystander citizen
in serious condition
on life support
induced coma critical condition
do not resuscitate tattoo
killed in action rest in peace
only 22 shopping days till christmas
all sales final
everything must know
open casket closed to family
in lieu of flowers
please read your bill of rights
cash bar no tabs
tax overhaul
quadruple bypass
debt ceiling credit extended
home for the holidays
universal health care dead on arrival
credit over-extended
check's in the mail
patient revives momentarily with selective amnesia
i don't recall i don't recall i don't recall
booze now cheaper than water
drugs cheaper than food
patient lingers as vultures hover
no hope no change
too wound up to notice
get your fresh
red hot organ donor stickers
does anyone here have a heart?

what's the rush amerika?

          where's the hurry
    a body only has so much time
a nervous system can only take
so much worry

you aim too low when you sell yourself
to buy things that keep you working
for 10 cents a dance

but it's never your dance & all you got
in the end is two cents

you can't break free amerika
not when the bank owns your house
& land & car & credit card debt

you think you know
what a power grab looks like
you ain't seen nothing yet
              so what's the rush
     where's the hurry

a body only has so much time
a nervous system can only take
so much worry

making amerika great again (redux)

the evidence is mounting
the witnesses have flipped
the tapes in safe keeping
the last indictments
sealed & waiting

the probe almost done probing
the media keeps repeating
& somewhere they're mentally
measuring orange jumpsuits

the calm before the legal storm
a time to reflect how far afield
a population can be driven
with distortion & manipulation
& absurd promises
that cannot be delivered

every one of us susceptible
to the knee-jerk news of our devices
& half-truth perspective
every one of us corruptible
with a vice a slogan & a dream

huge news is knocking

on your consciousness amerika
a massive quake is coming to shake up
the masses & wake up
your pleasure island donkey
persistence of darkness

they tell you your dreams are safe
they say your swamp is clean
your water is fresh
your produce is triple-washed safe
& full of leafy green goodness

they say everything is fine
the stock market is strong & growing
the jobs more & more plentiful
when everything we need
seems just out of reach

it's okay they say we'll erase the mistake
nuke that part of the tribe you never
wanted to belong to

but then the plates shift & crash
& we wake to the break of a great seismic day
rating effects of richter vibrations
on decaying foundations
leading us into a new cosmic twirl

pause for reflection

time to look in the mirror amerika
how your trickle-down theory trickles back up
your underwear & into your own pockets

some magic trick to turn millions
into billions into trillions without paying
uncle sam a dime in taxes
look! the system's been hacked
i mean designed for debt
& empty promises

can you please squeeze some honesty
& generosity from plymouth rock?

can you play a melody of harmony
from the liberty bell?

what do we do with the slave owners
on mount rushmore?

do indian killers & treaty breakers
& white supremacists get a pass?

you better close a few loopholes amerika
your worst contradictions are showing

your past is mostly at half-mast
& i see excessive inflammation

by the time you read this amerika

the times will have already changed
maybe there's nothing left to recognize
& all this raging looks strange
it's the nature of time
it's the nature of change

sometimes what you say doesn't matter
because context shifts & transforms
what used to kill is good for you today
new reforms meet new norms
it's the nature of time
it's the nature of change

best choose a course to the future
& watch it come into view
won't take as long as you think
& won't be exactly what you thought
it's the nature of time
it's the nature of change

sometimes feels like thinking is a trap
we catch ourselves in again & again
another fake rate of exchange
it's the nature of time
it's the nature of change

CHANTS & RANTS

in praise of the universal

one world one people one government
one religion one currency one store
one computer one war

       one ketchup one sandwich one beer
one cheese one wine one mustard
one pie one art one artist

one movie one book one ice cream
one game one channel one song
one spice one name

       one car one color one race one blood
one sport one lipstick one phone
one super highway

one news one program one decider
one mother one father one brother
one sister one dream

       one class one school one fashion
one job one meditation one corporation
one nation one medication

       one tongue one word one voice
one stupor one choice one illusion
one institution one zero
one zero

we're number one!

we're number one with a bullet
we're number one in arms sales
we're number one in military spending
we're number one in police killings

we're number one in bankruptcies
consumer debt & national regret
hospital debt & hospital deaths
in pledging allegiance to a half-mast flag

we're number one in church ministers
& turning citizens into prisoners
number one in election spending lobby bribing
GMOs drug money & suicide surviving

we're number one in television channels
& do-nothing congressional panels
in highway deaths & gang murders
following orders & material hoarders

we're number one in government surveillance
in marriage divorce & golf courses
we're number one in obesity & indecency
& conspiracy & hypocrisy

we're number one in plea bargains
& flea market bargains
number one in mistrials & show trials
& even if you try it it's hard to deny it
we're always number one in denial

we're number one we're number one
we're number one in the world!

no child left behind

pledge allegiance to the system
where only the failing get a little help
& the rest of the class go from good
to average to a little above
hobo in your own hometown

because Ds get degrees
in the great dumbing down
                no child left behind
      no child left behind
hey your new credit application
has not been declined
if you need a lift up
we'll help pull you back down

you'll only be unhappy
                if you think too much
you're being groomed to consume
& fine-tuned for the middle of the road
in every workforce or playground
because Ds get degrees
in the great dumbing down

you got to get in line to stand in line
& stay in line between the lines
it's a no-brainer
with treats & whips
we've all become animal trainers
      no child left behind
             no child left behind

too much

too much food too much booze
too much war too much choice too much
bullshit too much news too much
traffic too much smoke
too many mirrors
too much disease too much work
too much greed too much need
too much fear too much
pain too much heat too much rain
too many deniers
too much freedom too much control
too much watching
too much crazy
too much lazy too much
regulation too much confrontation
too many military
too much abundance too much
redundance
too much something
too much nothing

too much everything
too much sun too much fun too
much money too much debt
too much speed too much regret too much
congestion too much indigestion
too much repression
too much dogma
too many dog whistles
too much ruse too much imitation
too much subordination too
much separation
too much condemnation
too much crave too much rave too much
mine too much grind too much

machine too much upstream
too much imbalance
too many cooks

too much can't too much won't
too much always too much never
too much forever too much sadness too much
madness too much fadness
too much eye
too much pie too many lies
too much incarceration too much
universe too much expansion too much
exposure too much institution
too much mass confusion
too much ego
too much go-go too much no-show
too much mojo too much religion too much
too much to let go too much indecision
too much friction too much fiction
too much collapse too much max
too many facts

style (in a nutshell)

climate change is heating up
temperature's rising & the water won't stop
the drugs so strong they won't leave us alone
the battle of the sexes danced us to a nexus
with more allegations than guns in texas
seems bad dreams amnesia & denial
never go out of style

money don't know gravity there's too much at the top
100 billion is the new million
                & trillionaire's the new crop
as the sun sinks slowly in the west we're a nonstop
pawnshop lollipop belly-flop sweatshop
newsflash: the homeless are the next middle class
seems bad dreams amnesia & denial
never go out of style

they turn schools into jails & jails into hotels &
hotels into cells for any excuse to turn the screws
& grind your mind & pay your dues
heaven looks more like hell
the president's a nut congress in a rut
bacteria rules our gut miss amerika's a slut
the police chief's a thief while time steals us blind
seems bad dreams amnesia & denial
never go out of style

what happened to shame & guilt? no use cryin
over oil that's been spilt
booze & doughnuts & russian roulette
everything tastes like a cigarette should
from timbuktu to hollywood all part of god's plan
it's all effin good no reason to freak or panic
everything's natural & organic

we're just cruisin for a bruisin on a planet
called titanic
seems bad dreams amnesia & denial
never go out of style

life's a death sentence & death sets us free
once upon a time they called that irony
cause we're chasing the clock
but the clock's catching us
space is spinning like a top in a widening gyre
climate change is heating up & we're fighting
fire with fire
seems bad dreams amnesia & denial
never go out of style

give me liberty (ding dong)

big brahma bull riding a bowl of ramen noodles
slurping oodles of drama minus a comma
& mia mama glowing rays of gamma
from blind boys of alabama reading
the birth certificate of barak obama
give me liberty not trauma
give me liberty not trauma

mosquito hawk up mosquito blackhawk down
rainbow tomahawk missile moscow
crazy talk shuffle bluffing handcuffing
the spitting image of pajama mama llama
i don't wanna be impaled on no impala
give me dollarama ding dong
give me dollarama ding dong

if nothing's right is everything wrong?
here today & soon we're gone
hari rama krishna dogma noodles karma
doodle dalai lama allah java lava
tijuana iguana flora fauna yokohama
melodrama bahama mamba futurama
prima donna ding dong
prima donna ding dong

give me electricity not toxicity
give me creativity not hostility
give me flexibility not rigidity
give me infinity not radioactivity
give me divinity not disability
give me liberty give me liberty
& give me breath

hope is a four-letter word

fuck hope! the new battle cry
fuck hope! hope is for dreamers not doers
fuck hope! they eat hope for breakfast
fuck hope! they smell weakness all over it
fuck hope! praying won't bring us peace
fuck hope! they're killing us with guns & drugs
        & chemicals & lies
fuck hope! hope doesn't vote
fuck hope! and your cheerleader mentality
fuck hope! hope doesn't have a military
fuck hope! you don't stand a chance
fuck hope! hope believes hot dogs are good for you
fuck hope! & your carrot promises on a stick
fuck hope! your wings are broken
fuck hope! things are gonna get ugly
fuck hope! hope goes down with the ship
fuck hope! don't let someone else
        do your heavy lifting
fuck hope! time to detach & have a laugh
fuck hope! you can't handle the handle of the truth
fuck hope! hope is a derangement syndrome
fuck hope! your corruption is limitless
fuck hope! abandon all who enter here
fuck hope! how much darker do you want it?
fuck hope! & your bright shiny happy
        delusional amerikan dream
fuck hope! you know what i mean
fuck hope! we need deeds not words
fuck hope! you can let it happen
        or make it happen
fuck hope! and the horse it rode in on
fuck hope! passive flaccid submissive excuses
fuck hope! hope is the lazy way out

camera obscura

we got smokescreens for the smokescreen
cover-ups for the cover-up & a crisis
for the circus that's building to a nexus

we got two dozen clowns in a revolving door
running round & round spinning
bad news into war
spinning stories to deflect & obscure
because chaos is the new world order
& there never ever was
a physical cure
for the human condition

we got unnatural natural disasters
piling up faster & faster while we debate
the best way to make a buck
on death & racist hate

we got hookers & playmates & porn stars
in private cars we got ex-wives & french fries
& russian spies dying of nerve gas
we got trade wars & foreign whores
& puppet-stores full of mockery
we got lion tamers & wall street gamers
& media blamers getting lamer & lamer
we got out-liars & in-liars & pro-liars
& little white liars hell we're mired in liars
whose pants are never not on fire

we got generals on benedryl & nepotism
on a stick & we got excitements & indictments
& righteous heightening uptightments

we got wife-beaters & lost leaders &
ex-cheerleaders & bottom feeders

& tax cheaters who don't know when to quit
all the best people in all the worst places
we got lawyers by the truckload
& tigers by the tail we got communication
overload & half the staff is going to jail
we got everything you need to run
a second-rate soap opera white house bimbo
apprentice reality show

hold on to your chinese hats kittens & cats
you can't make this stuff up

we got science deniers & bible belters
& mojo filters & everything normal
is slightly off-kilter but we got faster fighter jets
& secret internets & bombs to end all bombs
we got super-spies to spy on the spies
& eyes that can't see
a combover isn't the answer
we got leaks in our leaks & jesus freaks
& faux antiques & it's all understood
we got too much power under the hood

distraction is the new chain reaction
look look! not here over there

& if that doesn't work we'll set something else on fire
we can always use the extra smoke to manipulate
the folk
     we can always use the smoke
to stoke the fun house
hall of mirrors

the wasteland of

pillars & columns
of domes & tombs & cartoons
of documents & monuments
of power & fear
          & cowards
    & towers

of rose gardens & embryos
of intrigue & incest
of trying to justify the past
while skating on
the future
          of founding fathers
& slave owners & the lost tongues of mothers
of our original fathers

of forgotten history & making history
& ignored history & rewriting history

of supreme courts & supreme jesters
of lost statesmen & suffragettes
& all those one neglects

of scandals & burglars
of backrooms & trap doors
of political spin & cynical pivot
of under the table
& over
the counter
          of corruption & gumption
& theocracy & dishonesty
of government & betterment
& putting on a happy
arms race

one & too

too much food too much booze
too much war too much news
too much traffic too much plastic
too much smoke too much toke

too much disease too much trapeze
too much work too much pork
too much greed too much need
too much fear too much pain
too much heat too much rain

too much freedom too much control
too much watching too much detaching
too much lazy too much crazy
too much something too much nothing

too much talk & not enough music
too much blame & not enough shame
too much money & not enough charity
too much hunger & not enough thirst
too much medicine & not enough healing
too much busyness & not enough action
too much drink & not enough satisfaction

too much color & not enough dancing
too much vapor & not enough planting
too much criticism & not enough flow
too much collecting & not enough
letting go letting go letting go

russian fever

the winter of our discontent
& there's russian fever in the air

they're buzzin our spy planes
with bugs in his orange hair

they got rotten bots on facebook
& hackers in your notebook

they got their money in our laundry
& presidents in their pockets

they got rockets & narcotics
& their pinkies in our sockets

while we're so easily distracted
by the litter of bullshit on twitter

i confess they even got putin
quoting newton in the press

& the whole circus scene smells
like an unflushed dirty tricks mess

drug money buys a lot of muscle
for your hustle in the shuffle

from PC to DC & back to red square
damn straight pilgrim i declare

there's a killer flu on the loose
& a russian fever in the air

plastic plastic everywhere

there's plastic in the air
there's plastic in the clouds
there's plastic on the beach
there's plastic in the ocean
there's plastic in the explosion

there's plastic in the nets
there's plastic in the fish
there's plastic in the water
there's plastic in the fodder
there's plastic in the pipes
there's plastic in the stereotype

there's plastic in the can
there's plastic in the frying pan
there's plastic in the birds
there's plastic in the words
there's plastic in the food chain
there's plastic in your maryjane

there's plastic in the baby bottles
there's plastic in the water bottles
there's plastic in the diapers
there's plastic in the toys
there's plastic in your girls & boys

there's plastic in the bags
there's plastic in the ads
there's plastic in the surgery
there's plastic in the currency
there's plastic in your credit
there's plastic in the senate

there's plastic in the landfill
there's plastic on top of everest

there's plastic in the carnivorous
there's plastic in your french fries
there's plastic in your sandwich
there's plastic in the albatross
there's plastic in your collectibles
there's plastic in your indigestibles
there's nurdles in the turtles
all the way down

there's plastic in the phones
there's plastic in the snow
there's plastic in the cars
there's plastic in the doors
there's plastic in the cures
there's plastic in the moors
there's plastic in the carpet
there's plastic in anarctica

in the pacific there's a garbage patch
of floating plastic
bigger than mexico
38 million pieces of trash
massive waste
vast overflow of mermaid's tears

there's plastic in attachment
there's plastic in the fragments
there's plastic in the packaging
there's plastic in everything she said
plastic in the living
& plastic in the dead

landscape art

glaciers melting farmlands subdividing
drive-ins dying forests are falling
horses are cars farmlands are golf courses
skyscrapers rising prairies burning
lakes are drying rivers flooding
the infinite is aging skies are crying
landscapes changing landscapes changing

roadways spreading sidewalks setting
wood barns collapsing grasslands ebbing
old growth dying oceans rising
fires raging tundra thawing
landscapes changing landscapes changing

the climate flowing people are moving
plates keep shifting future is drifting
spaces shrinking airports expanding
wetlands draining deserts growing
cell towers multiplying pollution appalling
the suburbs sprawling ravens complaining
traffic is jamming daybreak breaking
landscapes changing landscapes changing

waste is mounting clear cuts haunting
our wires crossed the past is lost
haystacks are history the caboose a mystery
the penny retired newspapers expired
winds are howling trees are bending
humans are fouling fires raging
denial fading but the air doesn't care
if the smoke keeps invading
with or without you the past is disappearing
with or without you turner keeps painting
time & space never stops destroying
& creating with or without you
landscapes changing landscapes changing

in spite of the spite &

the unknown hindsight of noses
& choices of moses & ourselves
we sometimes fight to fight through
the haze & fuse of the booze
& blues to pay our dues
for the screws to tighten the coffin
& every so often shine the shoes
of our gravesite plight

in spite of the height of the almighty
we fuddle & duddle & muddle
befuddled
        juggle our puzzles
& smuggle our muzzles of morals
while the mud in the puddle
settles in our kettle
before it boils & bubbles
into toil & trouble
                in spite of the terabytes
of trite before the troglodytes
& luddites of clockwork bullfight
we crawled out of the soup
& into a 3-piece suit to help squeeze blood
from suburbanite parasites
& load buckets of pirated loot
for the rude uncouth society
of rising anxiety

in spite of the blight of uptight
& the distorted contortion
of fortune & emotion
we continue to blind ourselves with eyesight
instead of the priceless insight we might
in spite of ourselves
in spite of the spite

they say the tundra is thawing

which really means the tundra is no longer
& i wonder what repercussions await

if i bang on a drum will the drum even care
if i bang on a drum when no tundra is there

will this thawing create an awesome awing
will it release the beast? no one knows just yet

it's too soon to remember & too late to forget
but tonight i declare there's a wonder in the air

because no one really knows what the world
will be like without any tundra to share

if i bang on a drum will the drum even care
if i bang on a drum when no tundra is there

hope you feelin better

feelin good feelin better
open another case
of climate change weather

feelin good feelin better
it's the amerikan chase
just to stay in place

feelin good feelin better
i'm hopelessly addicted
to the smell of her sweater

feelin good feelin better
we all wanna to feel more
inspired than before

feelin good feelin better
misery loves company
so let's get together

feelin good feelin better
it's the best song to sing
at the end of your tether

not my circus not my monkey

not my government not my president
not my bloody country tis of thee
not my movie not my role
not my news not my anchor
not my religion
not my guru not my school not my teacher
not my jungle not my zoo
not my job not my boss
not my profit not my loss not my doctor
not my nurse not my bank
not my purse
not my cell phone not my selfie
not my DNA not my blue jeans
not my music not my muse not my cross
not my jesus not my congress
not my gain not my loss
not my supreme court not my artificial heart
not my bill not my law not my resolution
not my persecution
not my mail not my prison not my hell
not my heaven not my cloud
not my jail not my god
not my police
not my dream not my scene
not my circus not my president
not my belligerent country tis of thee
not my monkey not my monkey
not my circus
not my monkey

some people

some people shouldn't be left
to their own devices

some people need constant supervision
some people could use a wake-up call

some people don't have a clue
some people tweet without thinking

some people can't accept defeat
some people don't know how to apologize

some people need a time out
some people have no compassion

some people need more heart expansion
some people are too full of themselves

some people are hurtful bullies
some people could use a few vices

some people shouldn't be left
to their own devices

the more he digs

the deeper he goes
diggity diggity dig
he cannot stop digging
himself into a hole
diggity diggity dig
he won't listen
to his advisers' advice
he's a man on a mission
with a shovel & a coverup
& an urge to purge but
he can't shut himself up
so he diggity diggity digs
& the more he digs
the deeper he goes
into the hole
his whole family flows
how big is that dig?
nobody knows
diggity diggity dig
he'll never strike paydirt
but chances are
he'll lose his shirt
diggity diggity dig
& he'll never move
enough earth around
to save his presidential crown
or cure his heartburn
don't look now
but he's past the point
of no return
diggity diggity dig

mantra for amerika

it's gotta get worse before it gets better
it's gotta get worse before it gets better
it's gotta get worse before it gets better
it's gotta get worse before it gets better
it's gotta get worse before it gets better
it's gotta get worse before it gets better
it's gotta get worse before it gets better
will we survive the terror of weather?
it's gotta get worse before it gets better
it's gotta get worse before it gets better
it's gotta get worse before it gets better
it's gotta get worse before it gets better
it's gotta get worse before it gets better
or will we wear the bitter scarlet letter?
it's gotta get worse before it gets better
it's gotta get worse before it gets better
it's gotta get worse before it gets better
it's gotta get worse before it gets better
it's gotta get worse before it gets better
it's gotta get worse before it gets better
it's gotta get worse before it gets better
it's gotta get worse before it gets better
it's gotta get worse before it gets better
how much more worse until we burst?
it's gotta get worse before it gets better
it's gotta get worse before it gets better
it's gotta get worse before it gets better
it's gotta get worse before it gets better
it's gotta get worse before it gets better
it's gotta get worse before it gets better
& it will get better & better & better &

the new improved blame game
(reality TV for paranoiacs)

blame mexico blame muslims blame immigrants
blame refugees blame obama blame regulations
blame scientists blame environmentalists
blame health care blame hillary
blame teachers & preachers
blame the military blame generals blame CIA
blame FBI blame the poor blame the left
blame europe blame the attorney general
blame judges blame puerto rico blame iran
blame north korea blame amazon blame china
blame the media blame NAFTA
blame opioids blame athletes blame leakers
blame tweakers blame students blame teachers
blame the UN blame NATO blame dreamers
blame protesters blame congress
blame crazy people blame fake news
blame the lawyers blame the law
blame women blame abortion blame liberals
blame radicals blame the deep state
blame voters blame disloyalty blame blame
sez the blamer-in-chief
blame the movers & shakers blame the makers
& takers blame the weak & poor
the old & infirmed the young & naive
blame the dim & crippled the sightless & senseless
blame blame blame enough blame
to go to the moon & back & still nothing changes
the same old blame & complain game
feeds on the failure of others but what about you
what did you do there's plenty to go around
but don't blame me because i blame you

when the boys-in-blue start wearing black

& act as if they want their money back
you'll have to pay one day or another
what happened to the world of color
& all those safer shades of blue?

suddenly their cars turned black
their windows their boots & belts & guns
& cuffs & glasses & hearts turned black

they're threatening they're menacing
they're mostly military surplus & rejects
trained to occupy & survive
not serve & protect

they'll kick your door down & shoot to kill
it's not about a conversation
it's just another clean up situation
to feed the morgue or the jail machine

suddenly their cars turned black
their windows their boots & belts & guns
& cuffs & glasses & hearts turned black

no such thing as a padded cell or honest bail
today it's a bloody awful dangerous fate
to be born without a silver spoon
in a brave-new-world police state

some things are looking up

obesity up suicide up medications up
video games up violent crimes up
wild fires up prices up credit card debt up
racism up temperatures up opioids up
conspiracy theories up e coli up
pollution up human population up
deforestation up refugees up anger up
animal waste up water levels up
hate crime up lost time up
unfrozen tundra up plastic waste up
earthquakes up tornados up
tailgating up potholes up road rage up
gun sales up hurricanes up
medical expenses up amnesia up
arrests up plea bargains up
prison population up frustration up
greed up poverty up billionaires up
bankruptcies up over-fishing up
gambling up divorces up heart attacks up
insomnia up mass shootings up
lack of attention span up
sadness up cell phone radiation up
take-out food up red tide up
oil spills up traffic jams up
depression up propaganda up
military spending up pornography up
low wage jobs up emojis up
camouflage underwear up
bald-faced lying up
texting & driving up impatience up
political distrust up
giving up
up up up & away

the energy-saving soul-sucking lights

the cheap booze the easy opioids
the rigid religion the flexible frame
the pursuit of happiness
the boob tube the portable computer
the incredible inflatable insatiable
the bloodless violence the deafening silence
the multitudes of heartless smart phones
welcome to the great stupor

the soft machine hard-liners
the new ex-vet old timers
the mindless banter of intolerant ranters
the benders the blenders the tenors
the contenders the pretenders the censors
the offenders the defenders the mentors
the lenders of dead-enders
& the suspenders of disbelief
welcome to the great stupor

the great amerikan numbing
the dumping the plumbing
the dumbing sideways & down
the pervasive dulling the full aimless
shiftless listless static humming
the nerdy geeks & herds of sheeple freaks
the stoner loners the sadistic addicts
the blind skeptics the non-stop rumors
the exponential tumors of consumers
the endless computer radiation
from lack of inspiration
the forgetful radical
the impractical animal
welcome to the great stupor

when is a poem

when is a fact not a fact when is
a lie not a lie when is a vote
not a vote when is a wall not a wall
when is a democracy not
a democracy

when is a crime not a crime when
is a russian not a russian when is a deal
not a deal when is a tax cut
not a tax cut when is a cage not
a cage when is a war
not a war
       when is a dollar not a dollar
when is a promise not a promise when
is an emergency not
an emergency

when is a joke not a joke when
is a crime not a crime when is a racist
not a racist

when is a witch hunt not
a witch hunt when is a pardon
not a pardon when is a president
not a president when is
a president
       not a president

resist!

upside down inside out outside in
all around & round about
this topsy turvy wavy curvy world
is making twisted fantasy
a far cry from what it used to be

i apologize for painting reality
so dim & dark i'm sure it's a trick
of the light or just a world gone wrong
the wrong people in jail
& the free fly out of control
or under the spell of a living hell
horror is our current structure
built on power for more power
& not for the people

the guard towers tower over us
with dog whistles of fear in the air
so we must blindly obey
their jackboot rules
or pay the piper forever
how do we declare our independence
from the veil of sweeping surveillance?
how do we break free from soul-crushing
taser-zapping handcuff control?

resist! their sideways bribes
resist! their false freedom carrots
resist! the faux promotion illusion
resist! their machines of manipulation
their inverse perversion of love
& doublespeak spirit
resist! their money-grubbing media
resist! the friendly noose of loose rules
they place around your neck

resist! the rope the bait before too late
it's for your own good they say
resist! the bars & chains
the shackles & heckles
from the bully pulpits of decree
i insist i insist we must resist!
resist! resist!

we got more groceries than poetry

we got comic books for adults
we got novels with more pictures than words
we got movies that teach you how to make a bomb
we got eight mcdonald's in vietnam
we got rainbows for gay pride
& unicorns for the transgender side

we got schools for billionaires
& the gutter for the poor
we got empty churches & prisons full
we got air you can't breathe
& water you can't drink
every night when our heads hit pillows
we got way too much to think

we got a dozen deep fried twinkies
& a barrel full of monkeys
we got gods doing odd jobs & angels
frozen in the architecture
we got frogs in our voices
& everyone wants a turkey leg up
we got dogs in our hot dogs
we got ketchup on our ketchup

we got too many cars & not enough bees
we got the best stress in the world
we got cones of chocolate & vanilla swirled
we got trigger-happy policemen
we got students who can't pay attention
we got five-thousand friends on facebook
we got the london bridge in arizona
we got a minifridge in the minivan
we got more heart attacks than lovers man

we got more coke than cola
we got more clocks than time
we got more problems than solutions
we got more delusions for our institutions
we got more groceries than poetry
we got more dollars than sense
we got more balls than brains
we got more military than intelligence

we got more than we know
& less than we realize
we live as though there's no end
to the bordeaux
& the infinite blue skies
but you never know when it's time to go
you never know when your last breath
comes & goes

EXHALES & DOVETAILS

aftermath

when nothing adds up
& there's too much pain & chaos
after the destruction

too much to figure
for feedback or equation

so you simply try to survive
& make each breath count
without counting

because you're too numb

to put a number
on what just happened

tip for amerikans

sit with yourself in stillness

turn off the gizmos & gadgets
those ubiquitous screens
& buzzing bulbs of terror

turn them all off
& listen to your thoughts

who is doing the thinking?
who is having this dualistic experience?

happy unhappy high low hot cold
rich poor material spiritual
body soul calm storm
none of it real

you are already holy
a god or goddess divine

you do not need to go anywhere
chase or flee anything
do or get anything
except

listen to the silence
listen to the silence

dust the edges of

the ledges of your kindness
clear the cobwebs of your consciousness
dive into your ocean mind
empty your trash
          let go of the cache
sit for a bit without chat
or byte

forget about regret & all that rot
take a ride inside on a higher plane
take an imaginary train
of no-thinking
thought

because third-eye vibration
is the new medication

your true intention
becomes your next creation
the further inside the deeper the ride
the higher you fly
the more you rise above
the disguise
          of pie in the sky
    of blood in your beer
& mud in your eye

the most revolutionary action is

not war or violence or debate
or declaration but
calm

the system knows how to defeat violence
but it cannot conquer calm

calm has all the power

no lashing no bashing no trashing
calm solves every problem

no time no karma no samsara no dogma
you can begin to start winning
at the beginning
with calm

no impulse no complication no instigation
calm puts you in control

no delusion no confusion no worry
no duality no burning concern
for income or outcome

no tomorrow no sorrow no problem
simply calm simply cool collected

deep breath calm

doughnut pain

i feel your hippity hop-head meth-mind
casino wino ice cream dark chocolate
scotch bonnet magic omelet mindset
your kool cigarettes & hedonistic tourettes
with gallons of diet pepsi dr. pepper
dr. feelgood better best crackerjack
prozac six-pack laugh track
heartbreak keepsake mandrake milkshake
half-baked rainbow cake consciousness
spinning into a million galaxies
of fantasy rhapsody & never enough

i feel your smoother higher fuller super flavor
your queen-size triple shot americano congo
of nicotine mercedes benzedrine adrenaline tonic
& gin extra-thin barbequed boot camp sleeping pill
fast food altered mood decomposing
fear & loathing leaving las vegas strip mall
whipped cream slipstream dream scene
homemade fade away jump shot
boom! goes the dynamite

> *i feel the endless fire of unsatisfied desire*
> *i feel the need for greed from see to shining sea*
> *i feel the surreal of feeding my face to erase*
> *every trace of this titanic amerikan stain*
> *i know we've gone too far again*
> *i feel your doughnut pain*
> *i feel your doughnut pain*

i feel the debt & weight of your extra hard
lemming herd cradle to graveyard 25%
interest charge credit card rash of stash in dough
& cash & the obscene smokescreen green

of the new wealth machine routine
caviar jet-set emotional support peacock schlock
your vodka scampi linguine lamborghini
driving you into the howard hughes
cat & mouse poor house of voodoo tattoo gurus
on a booze cruise heart bruise late payment
hot pavement & cold-blooded
perpetual billie holiday toot dust blues

i feel your paranoid opioid underjoyed
rag tag zig zag spoon fed horse-head
morphine blue jean jelly bean hipster scene
strychnine mainline needle track coco-puff
big flake nose candy party powder handcuff
street walker fast talker flunky junkie
drug hustler sugar pusher soul crusher
wasted laced spaced & shitfaced crank it up!
crank it up! i feel your teenage outrage
lost wage pupa stage rat-mazed
baby-faced gloomy juvee angst

> i feel the endless fire of unsatisfied desire
> i feel the need for greed from see to shining sea
> i feel the surreal of feeding my face to erase
> every trace of this titanic amerikan stain
> i know we've gone too far again
> i feel your doughnut pain
> i feel your doughnut pain

i feel your mushroom cloud psilocybin
lost horizon desert island peyote button blast-off
inside your magic muffin seeking insect speaking
mescaline feasting acid peaking
furry freaking teaching screaming weeping
speeding reaching for meaning & healing

everything breathing on the ceiling
& nothing but nothing can bring you down

i feel your fresh bread cheesehead pizza-fed
brownie munchie crunchy nutty
mango chutney tasty curry danish pastry
incredible edible fifth dimension
laughing grass mystic cookie
pie hole jelly roll apple fritter maple bar
boogie nookie sugar-glaze bavarian cream
emotional eating gorging purging surging
splurging merging sacred & profane
rollercoaster doughnut hole pain

> *i feel the endless fire of unsatisfied desire*
> *i feel the need for greed from see to shining sea*
> *i feel the surreal of feeding my face to erase every*
> *trace of this titanic amerikan stain*
> *i know we've gone too far again*
> *i feel your doughnut pain*
> *i feel your doughnut pain*

historians at the smithsonian say

over the last 100 years the size of doughnut holes
is getting smaller

                pastry experts believe
        the amerikan doughnut
has become less about
dunking
& more about delivering
colors & sugar

tradition in transition

other confection aficionados point out
doughnut selling chains in mass production
have standardized the size

whatever reason or rationale
        a dozen doughnut holes
                ain't what they used to be

the amerikan way strikes again:
reducing without reduction

as history erases itself

they say

they say you make your own face
they say you can change your DNA
they say you get the government
you deserve

they say this planet is a matrix
of interconnected control
the aliens have been here for years
& they come in at least a dozen races
through portals & wormholes & meatballs
they say inter-dimensional travel
is the next vacation destination
all aboard for the fifth dimension
in the 1960s

they say the universe is expanding & infinite
they say there are enough galaxies
for each earthly human
to own 25
if you could only find
a cheap flight around the universe
the price of real estate
would be significantly reduced
they say there's a parallel universe
& possibly no limit
to how many universes there might be
therefore it's logical to assume
your problems are small
so enjoy them while you can

they say your soul is eternal
your astral body floats around forever
& you can end your suffering by non-attachment
while you retire in luxury
with the right long-term investments

yet lottery winners
overcome their initial euphoria
& become depressed & more miserable
than when they were poor

they say the wealthiest want to shrink
the population
with extreme prejudice
they say competition is healthy & altruism
is never altruistic
they say war is inevitable
they say climate change is melting the poles
& shifting the weight of the world
yet for us
the last ten pounds
are still the hardest to lose

they say perfection doesn't exist
but if it does it cannot last for long

they say we all have untapped powers
they say our sun will burn itself out
they say the number eight is misunderstood
they say green is the color of ambition
money jealousy & art
      all artists are gamblers
when seen from outer space the sun is green
& they say if you can write one poem
that's remembered for 100 years
you're finally a success

they say you can't count to a billion in one lifetime
they say genetic memory goes back at least
four generations
they say do your life work

& you'll know who you are

they say god is everything
they say nothing is everything
they say god is dead
they say godot never existed
they say waiting
is another kind of arriving
they say the most important discovery
by mankind is zero

they say your life is both meaningless
& meaningful but i'm always confused
about which is when

they say time travel began in the 1970s
& the future has already happened
they say jesus never said i shall return
that was macarthur or terminator

they say brainwashing is the cheapest revolution
they say brainwashing a population
to embrace or accept war
is the greatest crime
they say without debt there could be no money
they say brainwashing is subtle
& systematic & you must
remain vigilant

they say there's no right or wrong answer
questions beget questions
convincingly they say
there might not even be any answers
they say they can speak
to the dead

but they don't talk to their neighbors

they say almost 50% of eligible voters
didn't take the time to vote
they say the two-party system is broken
& corrupt
      & as far as parties are concerned
no one's having a lot of fun anymore
they say if voting made a difference
they wouldn't let you do it

they say everything's in flux
they say everything's in flux
they say everything's in flux
in flux in flux they say everything's
in flow in flow & flux
everything in flux & flow
they say everything is changing
changing changing
for better & worse or worse & better
& there's less & less & less
but more to believe

they say everything is vibration
our spaceship is crashing
control is illusion
& it's darkest before the dawn
they say be more water
less rock

they say it's a one-time liquidation sale
everything must go
the end is near
& there's nothing to fear
they say art is what you can get away with

& if that's the case i definitely want
my money back

they say this poem was over a long time ago
perhaps on a thursday evening
much like this one yet in 1920
but who can be certain?
with quantum physics they say
anything is possible
anything is possible

how mediocre do you have

to get before you're always
at your best?
                    personally
     i never try too hard
because no one gives
you extra credit for extra effort

quite the opposite

quieter softer more discreet
to ease into the world
with as much grace
as possible

grace that doesn't grow on trees

must be continuosly cultured
nutured inspired
& refined

the anti-minimalist artist

added to take away
& then added some more

crossed out words to make sure
people would read them

painted over paintings
& painted them again

dripping paint crooked lines
always leaving a gem behind

he added to take away
& then added some more

a pattern of fallen paint
bright colors high contrast

a new language that spoke
to street & tower

he added to take away
& then added some more

storms are the drivers of change

& there's a trainload of commotion
barreling down the tracks so fast
it can't turn back

it's eating up the scenery
mangling & mashing machinery
because there's warm water to ride

a wave a surge a whirl a tide
caught in a massive swirl of flood
& beach & blood & breach

there's a fluid side to hearts & minds
surfing a deluge of flotsam & confusion
a magic whirlpool inside

the rumbling tumbling bubbling
churning turning troubling cauldron
of change coming soon

to your home home on the range
that faceless fearless train
where reckless driving rain

meets twisted chaos & collapse
perhaps the beginning of the end
till it drives change home again

you can't stay in the same

place forever
the past the present
the future
     all gets swept away

there's nothing like a perfect flash
that lasts for the better
there's nothing like a taste
of nostalgia for later

you can't stay in the same place
by saving face till the end of time

it's almost carved in stone
that when you find yourself
alone
     you got to move forward
     you got to move on

the past the present the future
all gets swept away

history is now

don't wait for tomorrow
it doesn't wait for you
nothing waits
it always changes
history is now

you'll never get
another chance to grab
this moment again
the past is always gone
history is now

life doesn't happen by itself
but it will if you let it
or you can just
let it go
history is now

every instant
a new chapter offered
a chance to rewrite our future
fact or fiction or mission or vision
it doesn't matter because
history is now

don't let them fake you
out of making it for yourself
take it shape it awake it
history is now
history is now

both

the system is both problem & solution

the solution is both answer & question

the question is both problem & answer

the answer is both system & problem

the problem is both answer & system

the system is both problem & solution

our isms are at odds

with our quantum
our phantom fields out of reach
our answers don't understand
the questions
                our solutions don't realize
       the heart of matter is beyond
our eyes & mind

there's no finality in reality
no end point to point toward

everything part of the continuum
cycles of circles curl & swirl
within & without

problem solution problem solution
no between or twain
        all evolving & dissolving
            into always becoming

our isms at odds with our awesome
everything forever rearranging
itself for change

progress

we got meetings to make meetings
to hold meetings to talk about
meetings to schedule meetings
to talk more about the future
& we call that progress

we got experts to make sure
our experts are expert enough
to carefully check
the expertise of our experts
& we call that progress

we got stories about stories
about real things they call a hoax
we got 57 ways to slice the truth
we got jobs but no work
we got work but no jobs

we got everything you want
& nothing you need & we always call
that progress
                  this ain't a test baby
          it's a real live situation
subject to change & turn on you
without your permission

here we are & there we go
again & again coming & going
unable to maintain status quo
yet able to go nowhere
& still we call that progress

grab the tail by both hands

keep yourself open to change
stay flexible be fluid
don't wait till it's too late

the best policy is generosity

try not to manifest
beyond your means

all ideas have a shelf life

factor in decay & disillusion
don't wait until it's too late

music makes music makes music
makes music
be fluid
stay flexible
absorb the wisdom of trees

keep yourself open to change
be fluid be fluid stay flexible

the best policy is generosity

remain a work in progress
candlelight will forgive you

don't wait till it's too late

telescope or microscope

either way the view is dope
you can't escape the scope of things
the simple ripple & the great hope of beings
the wave & rave & article of particles
the part of a heart breaking apart
& coming together on a wing & a prayer
of pressures & pleasures

every chorus of breeze that sings
through a forest of trees
& all the degrees of ease & disease
all the highs & lows
all the thawing & awing of unfreezing seas
all the fractions & factions
all our actions & directions
our retrospections & reflections
from the smallest quark
to the largest quirk
we're all dated & fated
infected & selected
all related & connected

how the whole creates itself
& we feed off each other from the slightest light
of thought to the greatest waves of might
how we make our energy from collective synergy
& create our space with how we wake
vibrations from near & far

the etiquette of regrets

we're all full of advice
we don't follow ourselves

it's just the way we're made
to hope others won't disappoint
as much as we have

      damn amerika you inspire
& depress me

all your promise & potential
yet all the profane detours
along the way

try to keep your standards high
& your digressions few

try not to underachieve
even though achievement
is a standard we set

from our own regrets

better than amerika

      i know a place she said
that's better than amerika

everything is better there
including all the weather there
the ocean the beaches the food
even the water & air

& everything is affordable
if you can make your life
portable
      nothing is very far
you don't need a car
you can walk everywhere
by stairs to a star

there's anything everything
or nothing to do
the beer gives me a buzz
& reminds me of you

      last but not least
the people & dogs & police
are much friendlier there

what the hell
are we doing here?

blinded by hindsight

they say it only takes three breaths
to let any thought go

but if you elect
······the wrong president
··it can take four years
··to let go

····some relationships
····take longer to fully let go

& others spend lifetimes
working the kinks out

seems we're better
at attaching than detaching
seems we're better at voting against
than choosing
for

how can i sell myself?

she sez everything will be all right
but it never is
& yet
      i still believe her

she sez each moment is infinite
so don't worry be happy & get ready
for big news

i wonder how good is good enough
& she sez all you need is one good deed
one painting one poem one joke
one song one photo one home run
at the right time
              to be remembered

she sez amerika sells herself
as a dream you can buy with your life
but when you wake up
there's nothing to get except
what you give

how can i sell myself
when i don't know who i am?

she sez work on yourself first
& all will fall into place
but as i do
everything keeps falling apart

she sez everything will be all right
but it never is
& yet
      i still believe her

stupor to stupor & dust to dust

the perfection of our perpetual stupor
how they trained us to sleepwalk through

the body-snatching effect of education
athletics employment indoctrination
marriage children & system
the zen of mind-numbing times ten

      stupor to stupor & dust to dust
      stupor to stupor & dust to dust

we got less joy from more toys
we got more highs & less rise
we got less funny with more money
we got more yo-yo & less mojo

they made sure we were disenfranchised
disengaged & scattered in divide
& conquer disarray
                       we used to believe
    we could change the world
give peace a fighting chance & not fall into
the same grinding machine as our parents

but the clockwork world ate us alive
the minute hand held us in our seats
day after month after year
we got fed the same lie enough times
a digital watch looked like a victory

we traded one stupor for another
tricycle for bicycle for car for truck for bus
for plane for train for jet for submarine
& dreams of a rocket-ship to mars

stupor after stupor after stupor
until it was too late & we realized
all stupors lead to loneliness
waiting in our cages to die

    stupor to stupor & dust to dust
    stupor to stupor & dust to dust

but not as sad as it sounds
because stupor takes the edge off
convinces you to feel better & begin to believe
your ordinary contribution might help
someone write a decent obituary
as if the dull circular
routine of mundane existence
really made a difference

    stupor to stupor & dust to dust
stupor to stupor & dust to dust

what did we learn amerika?

there's nothing like time for a recap
to beat a long dead horse
but of course amerika loves repetition
the grand national hair-raising tail-chasing
of making the same mistake
over & over again

military might can maim & kill
but cannot break the will of a people
united against it

when your health care is unhealthy
it's time to humanize & revise

without a foundation of compassion
& education the house of freedom & dreams
will crumble & crash

prison is a poor excuse to make a dime
squeezing the down & out all the time

it's easier to put a politician in your pocket
than cram a camel through
the eye of a needle

the police need policing
i repeat the police need policing

when did resistance become a spectator sport?

from time to time the press must disagree
or the press is simply not free

a conspiracy is not a conspiracy when it's true
because when it's true no escaping
or faking or cover up will do

fake news is the news you don't want to hear
fake news is the news that doesn't fit to print

beware the elusive nature of truth
it's dubious incarnations & variations
will confuse & subdue you

nation building is a fool's errand
because a stable nation must build itself
from the inside out

the less freedom a country has
the worse the education

money breeds wealth & wealth creates
greed & greed gives birth
to discrimination

there's nothing like a recap
to beat a long dead horse
of course amerika loves repetition
the grand national hair-raising tail-chasing
of making the same mistake
over & over

cosmic amerika

everything you love & admire
is a projection of an exact reflection
inside you
    the wondrous reveal of a sunrise
    the endless power of the ocean
    the thousands of raging suns
    twinkling in the night

you too are as vast & stupendous
you too are directly connected
to the infinite & always have been

you are a labor of love & always will be
you are all the excitement & pleasure
of your favorite holiday times ten

& everyday you get better & better
as everyday you fall deeper
& deeper
    into the dream
    of dreaming yourself
    exactly as you are

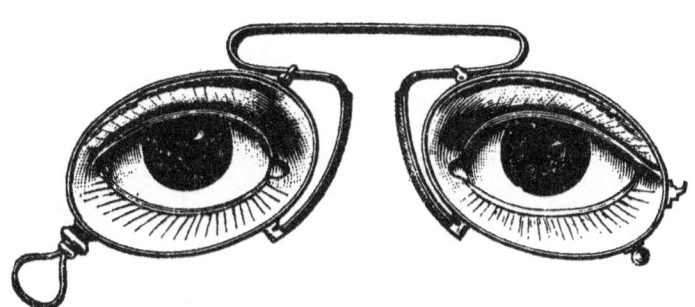

USA: PSA

#1 hazard

drinking cooking bathing water
breathing breathing air
indoor outdoor
workplace home
local coastal inland
global pollution is not a delusion
it's here there & everywhere
take care i swear
of your water & air
pollution is not the solution
take care i pray
of your water & air
nature holds the balance
of abundance
not man not money not meat
not greed for more
take care my young bears
of your water & air
pollution kills more than war
pollution kills more than war

the new climate models

are hotter than ever
this season
        ocean hemlines rising
intensifying storm patterns
of windswept waves
& tidal highs

while melting freshwater ice caps
worn tilted on axis
slow current circulation

warm muted colors of smoke & ash
will be the rage
        although
some eastern seaboard models
favor an eventual cooling trend
sporting brightly colored
turbo-down jackets
to herald the beginning
of greater seasonal extremes

whatever changes in the weather
brace yourself for complex
consequences
& make sure you're smartly garbed
in comfort & style

the insurance man

has a brand new company
with a brand new
plan
                but the cost is too high
       you can't afford to live
anymore the storms
too big & too powerful
to be swept under a magic carpet
& whisked away
             they say the aftermath
      down there looks like
a warzone
      they say the flood is everywhere
& the probability of uncertainty
becomes more likely
everyday
            they say everything
     falls apart to come together stronger
but only so many times
before you see the underwriting
on the floor

they say everybody dies someday
so always bet on chaos
always bet on
chaos

world war 3 or 5

has been raging for years
& most of us are
oblivious

in fact we don't even know
if it's environmental
or psychological

or under the radar
in cyber-space

we simply go about
our daily routine
              without a thought
       of the body count
or battles won
& lost

lack of awareness
great comfort

in these trying times

sleepwalking

we gave ourselves the mark
& we created the beast

big brother has the toys to watch you
& watch you they do

>   the chip in your card
>   the GPS in your car
>   the text on your phone
>   the cameras on the street
>   the speakers have ears
>   the internet trail
>   of browsing crumbs

that brother's been watching you for years
all that's left is thought-control
seems they got it covered
in our dreams

we're sleepwalking with the beast
& we don't want to wake up

we're sleepwalking with the beast
& there's no turning back

we're sleepwalking with the beast
& we don't want to know

disorder syndrome

disease mongering is a new disease
that's spreading from drug companies
to doctors to patients

until half the country suffers
from some made-up medical journal
big-pharma syndrome

                         the more we medicate
                   the less we meditate

we're mostly drugged up amerika
& happily dozing off into the sunset
of suicide or lethargy

wrapping ourselves in the rosy glow
of everything is beautiful horrible
violent & wonderful

                         the more we medicate
                   the less we meditate

more stars & bars & pills & stripes
we've become the zombies
of our games & movies

we replaced the art of self-coping
with universal doping
until clarity looks like insanity

                         the more we medicate
                   the less we meditate

it's not hip to shoot

even less hip to shoot from the hip
because you're bound to hit
your toes
               if you squeeze too fast just
like when you drink coffee
too fast
       it drips from your lips
& dribbles down your shirt
except that doesn't hurt
half as much
as losing your toes
or curse the woes of getting shot
up your nose

you know it's not hip to shoot
even less hip to shoot
from the hip

patriot act

the movie critic isn't anti-film
the food critic isn't anti-food
the book critic isn't anti-books
the art critic isn't anti-art
the gamer critic isn't anti-game
the music critic isn't anti-music

they love their chosen fields
& critique with passion
because they care

& those who criticize amerika
are not anti-amerikan
we're patriots

                  who can't stomach
          watching the best parts
of our country get trampled
dismantled & destroyed

facts will change

the NPR newscaster said
make sure you tune in
on a regular basis
because
facts & details will change

the facts they are a-changing
shifting & grifting
sounds like fake news to me
manipulated & proven wrong
right before our radio eyes

why no one trusts the news
why no one believes in the truth
anymore
cause there's a mad mad rush
to report it first

complete with facts that change
watch the game that keeps
you glued
to tuning into the new
conspiracy theory

take me to your leader

we got your ordinary garden variety
dictators & despots by the dozen
we got fake news narcissists
& puppets on a string
we got errand boys sent by grocery clerks
who'll fetch just about anything
we got sons & wives of former heads of states
we got speakers for bankers at dinners
for three-thousand-dollar plates
we got a loose rooski on horseback
baring his chest & nobel prize winners
who can't pass the test
we got billionaire communists
& strong men with limp wrists
we got a hundred senators & not one ace
we got 18 races of aliens from outer space
& repressed redneck preachers
too eager to fall from grace
we got corduroy cowboy actors
& steroid badboy sports stars
shooting from the lip
we got weekend warrior hawks
with more balls than brains
we got all kinds of crazy
in a power feeding frenzy
but where o where
have all the real leaders gone?
we got to find a few before we're done
find at least one before we're done

under control

the government knows
the biggest prison is your mind

& they want to keep you there
under their attentive care

so don't stray too far from the fold
they made for you to fall into

the government knows
the greatest freedom is your mind

& you can go anywhere
your imagination desires

so they build borders of fear
give limits & edges to your senses

how they induce to reduce you
how they cartoon & cocoon you

teach you to stay within reach
& feed you powders & pills

to keep your blood pressure
& power under control

news fast

a news fast they say
will reboot your internal drive
& slooow everything down

a news fast they say
will reduce fear & anxiety
& all your worry effortlessly

a news fast they say
will make you more optimystic
& generous & natural

a news fast they say
is an excellent resonant tonic
for your subconscious

someday a news fast will be
against the law
& you might be guilty as charged
for not getting wound up
in the mantra of propaganda

a news fast they say
will never disappoint you
or disjoint you

a news fast will give you
aesthetic perspective
more time for making art
& making love

an ounce of prevention

is worth a pound of cure
said the only amerikan renaissance man
but nobody listens to ben franklin
anymore unless we're talking
hundred-dollar bills

counting for inflation & appreciation
the prevention figure is 200 pounds by now
which suits big pharma just fine

ben touted beer for the working man
but he personally favored fine wine
one of the reasons he accepted
that ambassador gig
in france

no blood pressure pills back then
only the company of beautiful
french women
           speaking of prevention
      what a perfect military strategy
to tactfully avoid conflict
everyone saves face & everyone
saves their bacon

some things can't be avoided but
whenever necessary the path of prevention
will often make you look wise

the fourth of july fireworks

are made in china
the quiet giant country that owns
our economy
        & steals our intellectual property
        & manipulates their currency
        to give themselves an edge

their billionaire culture keeps growing
sowing seeds of communist greed

        they used to take our waste
        but that's beneath them now

they send us their orphan daughters
while they buy up our wine
& land
with an eye on the future
& their 1000-year plan

yet tonight
        the fireworks are pretty
        & we enjoy them
        while we can

life is a museum

fill yours with art
& memories of people you love

think of every object every tool
every experience every thought as art
or the potential to make art
& you'll curate a life
full of travel
challenge surprise & growth

when you grow old enough
your mind will be the main library
for your family

respect & cherish your museum
invite young people for conversation
teach them how to create
their own museum

show them how a small object
contains a universe
how a poem
can make a difference

how one life
can change the world

they're digitizing your future

art books music movies games news
everything streaming online
for your convenience
& their control

      life without a hard copy
is more than a little scary

whole catalogs can be erased
hit delete
& never seen or heard
or read again

as new regimes take power
history is always edited & revised

historic documents & manifestos
retouched photos
photo-shopped reputations
elevated & or destroyed
disappeared ghosted

save your originals & paper editions
keep them safe from harm
as if they'll be coming for them
amerika
      because eventually
      they will

another important warning

the most dangerous class
of fascism is capitalism

because capitalists lose perspective
& themselves in their work
eventually get caught up
in a vortex of greed

the natural character of the beast

as stockholders scream for more & more
& the captains of industry
tighten the screws

squeeze every last drop of life
out of worker & nature

until the only possible
conclusion
is war

USA: PSA (wake up! amerika)

#519
the art of health
must include a healthy dose
of art

#426
we seem more interested in
what killed the dinosaurs
than what's killing us

#841
organic non-GMO
kosher vegan junk food
is still junk food

#396
our war on wars are better
at dropping bombs than
planting peace

#553
you build your economy
on the foolish uncertainty
of permanence

#306
all the phallic symbols
in the world do not add up
to an ounce of compassion

#664
you have become
the dangerous aliens
you warned us about

#193
the more human we try to be
the more inhumane
we become

#504
the value of a dollar
depends on the values
of the country

#379
for every neon buddha
one-thousand crying
jesus tattoos

#1057
the richest man in the world
is not smart enough to refrain from
taking pictures of his penis

#023
give yourself the gift of emptiness
to make some room for clarity
& natural growth

#687
the president said
i've already kept more
promises than i've made

#889
stupidity & abuse of power
meet at the crossroads
of treason & silly season

#496
foolish norms
are the brainwashing glue
of high society

#058
the more you lie to yourself
the less likely you are
to tell the truth to anyone

#192
the best work inspires others
to use their imaginations to inspire
others to do their best work

#449
how do you tightrope
that fine line between
humanity & insanity?

#493
over 250 years later & the government
still cannot remove the fork
from its tongue

#731
a nap a walk a dream a thought
finish at least one thing
every day

#179
they only teach you
the things they want you
to know

#028
we learn to count
long before we can read
& that's how they control us

#491
wish i didn't have to ask
is human nature
an oxymoron?

#295
move from head to heart
& stay there
as long as you can

PRAYERS & FLARES

dear amerika your faith in

capitalism has become too dear
you created a class of crude & crass
      until we over-believe
in exponential greed

you've spawned the religion of never enough
you've splintered our energies
into the mutation
of instant gratification

you define great art by the fortune
it brings at auction

you've given everything a price tag
without realizing the value
of anything

dear amerika your money god
has run out of miracles
you've lost your way in a mythical maze
of vendors & lenders & biblical
distortions

      if only money could buy the end
      of poverty & snobbery

if only we could buy a bottle
six-pack or case
down the hatch to help us find our place again
to give us back our true spirit
ignite our luminosity
& awaken our generosity

dear amerika i pray for you

around the sun we spin

all our quicksand hurry
slipping through
this hourglass of worry
grain by grain by car by plane
the faster we spend time
we get further & further behind

you can't outrace time amerika
no matter how much matter
you say does or doesn't matter
everything must eventually change
& grow a little older & strange

2,000 years from now
will we still play that song
where everyone gets along
& nothing is wrong?
will we still want a home
on the range?

2,000 years from now
will they still sing your name
in the middle of the game?
will the dream
of a country with liberty
be long gone?

embrace your inner revolutionary

the genuine far-sighted visionary
the flexible philosopher poet
the outcast the offbeat
the out-of-the-box
wayward original thinker

be careful of company you keep

stay away from rigid prickly rule-driven
controlling bomb throwing
uptight mediocre minds

beware the dull dim-witted plodding leftover
far-right one-wing lack of humor man

don't follow the followers
the disciples of doublespeak
& desperate dogma
don't follow the factions of fear
& invaders of privacy
don't read the rewriters of history
don't follow the leaders of the followers
double-think double-think

the sheeple will destroy all hope

may the controllers & order-enforcers
stay fast asleep & out of your dream

prayer for amerika

when you collapse will you feel any pain?
writhe in agony? die a violent death?
ignite a new revolution or quietly
                              f-f-f-fade fade away

will you burn like rome or get cancelled
due to lack of interest?

will your power your dream be transferred
to another or will all countries become one
in global harmony?
                  not bloody likely

will you be reincarnated in a parallel universe
so you can learn the lessons
you failed to master the first time?
or will you crave cheeseburgers & fries again
football over books & virtual
over natural

i pray your death & rebirth are not difficult
seamless almost uneventful
not because i don't appreciate you
but because i do

i pray you make the history books
& stay there amerika

i pray mostly nice things are said about you
& some of your leaders are lauded
for profiles in courage & compassion
not rage or dashing fashion
because
        collectively
        you did try to do some good

when you weren't so full of yourself
when you made time & money
to help others

i pray you don't end up glorifying wealth & war
while some other country beats you
at your own game & the planet is destroyed
& we have to start all over again

i pray the spirit of your best generosity lives on
for the greater good & you change
your self-destructive ways
before it's too late

or do you think everything is inevitable
pre-ordained & born to die?

if they write you out of the history books
because of your idiotic patriotic
violent streak
            your religious genocidal
small-minded short-sighted bigotry
& your blind dysfunctional lust
for greed over natural order
we will deserve it
because all are not guilty
but we all share the responsibilty

i pray it's not too late to take
your intuitive ingenuity & change course
because great things can be done
for the right reasons

      yet the tipping-point
of no return is coming
at us fast

what to do

what you need to know
what you need to fix
what you need to make
what you need to grow
what you need at your fingertips

what you need to understand
what you need to be a man
what you need to be a woman
what to you need to make a catch
what you need to learn to earn

what you need to ease the pain
what you need to please
again & again
what you need when you
don't know what you need
is a friend indeed

youtube it
youtube it
youtube it

all the old barns are

falling down
        wood sold off to those
                who value the strength
& character of weathered boards
from old growth trees
hand-cleared
                by pioneer farmers
      centuries ago
to create & shape
their fields from rich forest
& riverbed floors

the river now receded
forest long gone
& the barns
another symptom of our disposable
amerikan aesthetic

                disappearing
        two by four
one by one

memo to future leaders

why force order when the natural order
is chaos?
        obsession with control
leads to defeat & disappointment

we are not heartless robots
seeking greater power battery life
until our warranty expires

        time is precious & finite
        time is sacred & holy
        time is not money

              what can you do
          before you must
        give your body back?

a little more attention to comfort & joy
a little more attention to education
& meditation
              a little more reflection
       & introspection

a little more attention to depth
of breath & breathing
better air

theory vs behavior

the unified theory of everything
is hard for humans
to imagine
                    because we get distracted
by atom bombs & god particles

to kill & create our nature
to classify & divide into subsets
of subsets
until we're silly busy
fighting over parallel universes
when we can't even get
one country right

        better to focus on why we're here
we'd create more time & space
& leave a better place
behind
                  the key to my equation
        is the perpetual vibration
of universal heart-expansion

thank god for the coast

both east & west beaches & ocean
& waves & birds of all kinds

too bad they all can't be california girls

thank god for ocean air & shells
moonrises & sunsets over water

thank god for the quiet power of clouds
their shade & shapes & shades
of color & calm fearless
floating nature

thank god for the greatest of great lakes
& summer sand between toes

thank god for deep green islands
purple mountain mysteries
& the blue sound of ancient waves
keeping civilization at bay

wave after wave after wave

when falling is our calling

this planet this country this life
always falling falling falling
                from one fall to another
& trying to avoid the fall leads
to a bigger one

better to look ourselves in the face
& accept our lack of grace
                realize we were born to fall
    & our mission to embrace
the stumble
                the only way to move forward
    lurching & stumbling
over ourselves
                    humans are erratic
              because nothing is static
      you can't stay in place
to attain perfect grace

when falling is our calling
when falling is our calling

this planet this country this lifetime
        there's no up or down
             just a perpetual stumble
              from one muddle to another
the best we can do
become a more humble stumble
falling falling falling stumbling
toward the future

when falling is our calling
when falling is our calling

a momentary lapse into optimism

we need to transcend our screens
before we devolve into machines of routine
vexed by text & autocorrect

we need to see through this milieu
beyond the smoke & vanity mirrors
of ones & zeroes & two-bit heroes

we need to rise up against the power
of sedate & hate & bait & banker
& divide to conquer

we need to break free of reality TV
& spin away into true actuality
there's no place like OM

we need to change & rephrase
transcend & mend & dervish blend
the material whirl into infinity

we need to make a place of grace
to cultivate a higher state & elevate
the art of heart & space

you know you're in trouble

when they burst your bubble
with three little words
that seem almost absurd
until they're spoken for you
while you're stuck in the muck
like a bear stealing honey
& you hear TV lawyers say
follow the money
follow the money

then you'll regret every cent
you ever made or spent
they'll cast a net so far & wide
you can't ever hide
from the hounds on your tail
things could get bloody
when you hear the refrain
follow the money
follow the money

they'll track you & your friends
they'll crack every witness
twist them against you
you'll wish you never did business
with anyone but your mummy
because everything's in question
as your world gets ugly
when they begin to repeat
follow the money
follow the money

earth justice is coming

at a speed you can't run away from
the beginning of the end
of a new beginning
           you can't kill the planet
     before she fights back

earth justice is coming
we're at the crossroads of fire & flood
& the blessing of cleansing
will be biblical
          we're at the crossroads
    of volcano & quake
& the chaos will be both
wonderful & wrathful

earth justice is coming
we brought it on ourselves
         placed profit over nature
     didn't listen to our mother
so we're at the crossroads
of science & religion
& we better get them together fast
because the cleansing will be
biblical
     both frightful & righteous

earth justice is coming
many old ways are dying
but you can't kill the planet
before she fights back

how do you know

when you're finally finished?
so hard to know when you're done

yogi said it's not over till it's over
but when has the next begun?

you might begin to repeat yourself
you might begin to repeat yourself

& get bored with this loopy routine
but there's always more work to do

      you gotta press forward
you gotta push through

a plateau is a sign to let it all flow
keep on working & then you'll know

when it's time to take a bow
it sure as hell ain't now

not with everything diminished
& every hour feels like a deadline

nothing's ever really finished
you just run out of time

please don't let your reptile brain

deceive you control you or make you
focus more on fear than love
because fear closes
          the doors of perception
    stops heart expansion
& stunts greater awareness

please keep an eye on
how they use fear to influence your vote
your buying habits your worship
your entertainment
your thought
patterns
      fear of a fear perpetuates the terror
      & you'll get stuck
      in their negative loop
      & manifest
      violence & dread

please grow out of your reptile brain
encourage the rewards
of courage
& create a life
where we help each other up
not separate or segregate
& drag
our neighbors down

please leave your reptile brain behind
be confident kind & sincere
& never ever let them
reduce your heart to fear

don't lose your sense of humor

1.
amerika don't lose your sense of humor
as you lose your global power

remember your humble beginnings
the first hungry thanksgiving
your valley forge fortitude
your lewis & clark character
your wagon train adventure

please don't forget your generous spirit
your helping hands
your humanitarian ventures
your sense of being in this together
with the rest of the world

please don't ever be bitter
or lose your sense of humor amerika
take a walk in the forest
& remember
we all come from nature
& return to nature &
it's healthy to laugh at yourself

2.
all empires corrupt & collapse
all dynasties dine on themselves
so don't take yourself too seriously amerika
give up the illusion of control
& give generously
to future powers that be

may they grow more openly more yieldingly
learn to be more water than rock

don't lose your sense of irony amerika
no country is as great or bad as its press clippings
eventually we'll get over ourselves
& dream a better dream soon
& build a cheaper energy-free hovercraft
& draw a funnier cartoon

untangle unwind chill out amerika
as long as we hold on too tight
the joke is always on us

3.
amerika loosen your tie your collar
your belt your purse strings
open your blackout redacted secret curtains
plant more trees & pump fresh air
from your smokestacks & chimneys

they say it's a game of inches
of rules & laws & flaws
they print in god we trust on our money
& pour our treasure & future
into the war machine
then ask us to pray for them
as if god authorizes our petty battles
or she's betting
on her own destruction

amerika don't lose your sense of humor
god is way funnier than you are
she knows all the punchlines
ahead of time
& lately her jokes are getting darker

amerika don't lose your sense of humor
it's one of your best qualities
humor will always pull you through
your self-imposed problems
& help you see the futility
of playing the heavy

4.
amerika lighten up
your meal deal family size super-duper
buckets of deep fried slop
topped off with let 'em eat cake & pie
& doughnuts by the mindless dining dozen
in front of your obesity TV gravy train
is broken down at the station

amerika don't suddenly
weigh yourself for shock value
you already know your once youthful trim
has expanded its girth to bases
around the globe

take a walk in the forest
& remember we all come from nature
& we all return to nature
& better to examine our issues with humor
because humor is our true nature

5.
amerika don't lose your place in history
by barking up the wrong tree

don't lose your mark twain buster keaton groucho marx
your will rogers carole lombard lenny bruce
woody allen george carlin

your jack benny henny youngman don rickles
rodney dangerfield bill hicks lucille ball
charles schultz r. crumb kurt vonnegut dorothy parker
your gahan wilson carol burnett robin williams
steven wright mel brooks gracie allen george burns
laurel & hardy firesign theatre
sense of humor
                learn to laugh again at yourself
        sharpen your wit on critics & politics
maintain your edge but don't abuse it
be critical without getting personal
we're all perfectly flawed
so nothing is funnier than failure

laughter vibrates longer & resonates stronger
than war & prison camps & death camps
& sweat shops & boot camps & work camps &
christian camps & corporate think tanks
that believe war is good for business
& the economy will set you free

laughter won't let you down
you can build a town on a mouse
& take the eternal vibration of laughter
to the ever-after

amerika don't lose your sense of humor
you'll need it when you least
expect it

lady liberty

as the world turns
& heads spin
& thoughts loop
& lives spiral
& planets corkscrew
& hearts open
& glasses empty
& refill
      the golden hour
gently kisses your cheek
while we chase the sun
around the universe
another year
everything changes
every second
nothing is ever the same
nothing
      except the shine
of your ageless patina
& my eternal
effortless
love for you

it's time to wake up! amerika

you got too many politicians in the kitchen
& not enough perception in the soup

you been breaking eggs for decades
& not one decent omelet yet

you can't stop chopping onions
& crying for all the wrong reasons

amerika you don't need to lose
those 20 extra pounds
you don't need to make more money
you don't need another makeover
or takeover or fakeover
you don't need a better deal
or another 60% off sale
you don't even need reality TV
you don't need another investigation
a clever quotation deeper penetration
stronger medication or instant salvation

amerika you need a daily meditation

you need to empty your collective mind
hit the reset button on religion
& capitalism & politics & education

let go of old habits amerika
your obsessions & addictions to power
& winning & taming & control

let go of that massive flag-waving ego
& fly your pride at half-mast for a change

expand your heart & head amerika!
a golf ball-size consciousness
produces golf ball-size awareness

free yourself from your self amerika
you don't need a bigger plane
a faster jet or a better helicopter
you don't need a brand new muscle car
or a davy crocket rocket to mars
when you realize you are the vehicle
& meditation is the fuel

slow down amerika
you are the destination
you are infinite & immaculate & immortal
the last frontier is inside you
& you can go anywhere you want

you can have what you want
if you want what you have

this is no joke amerika
this is not a test amerika
      awareness is everywhere
but you must first start
with yourself

may you live in interesting

rhymes
      may you live in a progressive mind
may you learn one great thing
that defines you
may you use your free time
to free yourself
again
      may you live in hoods
or woods
without coulds or shoulds
with more windchime than crime
may nature always be
greater
      may you never
           have to suffer war
or be so poor you can't find an open door
may you love in interesting
climes
may your juices flow with positive enzymes
may your mind always be in its prime
may you know how to read
between the lines
        may you have
        some breathtaking
    heartbreaking
climbs
may you give more than you jive
& set the pace with grace
may you love the life
you live
      may you live
in inspiring times

the aliens have arrived

they've been here for thousands of years
they can shapeshift to look
exactly like us
                    but deep inside
they're light years ahead

some are here to observe & monitor
some to subjugate & control
& some to help save us
from ourselves

       it's not hard to believe
in more intelligent life

amerikans want their saviors readymade
some other greater power
that magically divinely instantly
guides us to heaven on earth

when all along everything we seek
is inside us waiting
to awaken

let's change the world

sometimes you gotta laugh
because it's too damn dark
sometimes you gotta sigh
to keep from crying
sometimes you gotta smile
    & jump the shark
you gotta defy the odds
to leave a mark

    let's change the world
    one mind at a time
    you work on yours
    & i'll work on mine

but whatever goes down
don't ever stop trying
to focus on those flowing
oceans of consciousness
we'll build a righteous wave
of bottomless confidence
that rises as it grows
& creates more than it makes
& gives more than it takes
we'll turn momentum &
realization into total
transformation

    so let's change the world
    one mind at a time
    you work on yours
    & i'll work on mine

remember freedom

we will need people who can
still remember freedom

who understand why it's worth
fighting for not just fighting to fight
for the sake of fighting

we will need people who will not
tolerate totalitarian ways & means

who rail against humanity's handcuffs
& dead-end prison bars & systematic
thoughtless thought-control

who refuse to march in their endless war
or stand for unequal rights

we will need people who can remember
how to escape the oppression
of reprogramming

who can think & reason for themselves
yet act for the good of the whole

we will need people who embrace
the logic of natural magic
& create something extraordinary
out of nothing
                without destroying
the everything or the nothing
without becoming the destroyed

we will need people who can
still remember freedom

all portals   open

all systems go
everyone all aboard
time to expand
space to grow
    everyone dancing
  on the head of a pin
everyone groovin
let's do it again
    all portals open
    all systems go
      everything overcome
      nothing you can't do
  thy will be done
  thy will be done
    all portals open
    dive into the blue
    everyone all aboard
    layers of cosmos
    wait for you
all portals open
into universal stew
      old ways change
      old ways return
    get open into the flow
    only here & now
  & nowhere else to go
nothing else to do
spirits lifted up
& through
    into easy to be
  & synchronicity
  all portals open
all systems go

Stephen Roxborough is a native New Yorker transplanted to the Pacific Northwest. He grew up in the midwest in a pre-computer cold war better-living-through-chemistry duck & cover McCarthy witch-hunt black & white TV dinner howdy doody instant mashed potato atomic age.

He was weaned on the great American propaganda machine when presidents of either party were our heroes. The GOP was the party of Lincoln and FDR was a god in a wheelchair. We all believed our government was the force for good.

Then the 1960s happened. Assassinations, marches, protests, false flags, Kennedy conspiracies, our National Guard killed students, and even a real time murder on television.

The doors of perception opened & a generation walked through.

Bob Dylan, woman's liberation, civil rights, Haight Ashbury, orange sunshine, acid rock, Andy Warhol, strobe lights, birth control, Eastern philosophy, the British invasion, Carlos Castaneda, meditation, burning bras & flags & draft cards…

He watched the Vietnam War on the nightly news. Witnessed the rise & fall of Richard Nixon. Experienced the computer revolution. The introduction of robotics

& artificial intelligence & virtual reality. The rise & fall of the World Trade Towers. The Patriot Act. The age of billionaires & endless pointless futile wars. The death of privacy. The rusting of liberty. The continued lust for power & control.

You could say, he still remembers freedom.

additional poetry collections by stephen roxborough

the DNA of NHL (2017)

Ego to Earthschool (2017)

ode to radio nola (2017)

a beginner's guide to vital trivia (2016)

even bob dylan sometimes must have to
    stand naked (2016)

bob dylan's 853rd nightmare (2015)

drinking with the ghost of dylan thomas (2015)

open heart sutra surgery (2013)

luminosophy (2013)

this wonderful perpetual beautiful (2011)

son of blurst (2010)

blurst (2008)

impeach yourself! (2006)

so far all the very important mind-expanding
    long ones (2002)

spiritual demons (2002) CD

making love in the war zone (2001)

acknowledgements

Thanks to John Burgess, who bravely & generously took on a manuscript of over 475 pages & made keen editing decisions from a perspective I could not.

Thanks to Art Director extraordinaire, Milo Duffin. His expert eye and collaboration is invaluable.

Thanks to Dale Winslow, a more kind, bigger-hearted helping friend you'll never find.

Thanks to my mother, whose fierce independent immigrant love of country is baked into my DNA.

Thanks to my sons, Zak & Eli, who made me give a damn about the future.

Thanks to Dr. Swan who gave me incalculable cheer & encouragement through some hard, dark days.

www.ingramcontent.com/pod-product-compliance
Lightning Source LLC
Chambersburg PA
CBHW021951290426
44108CB00012B/1023